T0273319

STUFF
YOU NEED
TO
KNOW

A GUIDE FOR YOUNG ADULTS WITH AUTISM

Patricia Weaver, BS, PA

STUFF YOU NEED TO KNOW

All marketing and publishing rights guaranteed to and reserved by:

FUTURE HORIZONS INC.

721 W. Abram Street
Arlington, TX 76013
(800) 489-0727
(817) 277-0727
(817) 277-2270 (fax)
E-mail: info@fhautism.com
www.fhautism.com

© 2018 Patricia Weaver

All rights reserved.
Printed in Canada.

No part of this product may be reproduced in any manner whatsoever without written permission of Future Horizons, Inc., except in the case of brief quotations embodied in reviews or unless noted within the book.

ISBN: 9781941765913

CONTENTS

CONTENTS

UNIT 1 BEING HEALTHY

NOTES AND SUGGESTIONS

Being healthy is an important aspect of life that is relevant to everyone. Unfortunately, we do not routinely teach specifics about this part of our lives for several reasons. Often these are embarrassing subjects to discuss, or there may be other concerns such as medical issues. Regardless, young adults with disabilities need to better understand their own bodies and how to take care of them as they become more independent and start handling themselves as adults. Hopefully, this unit is a good starting point. We want these stories to open up an honest dialogue between the young adult with autism and their mentor, so issues can be openly discussed without embarrassment. Please understand that none of these stories are related to any specific person but are a representation of common occurrences I have learned through my extensive work with my own family and within the autism community.

In the section "Healthy Numbers," we discuss our weight, BMI, and how these numbers relate to our overall health. When we discuss weight, the number isn't as relevant as how we feel, whether or not we can participate in activities we enjoy, and our overall health. In "Active Lifestyle" we discuss how to get and stay in shape by staying active. As we age and leave the daily routines of school and team sports behind, it is easy to become sedentary and gain weight. We open the discussion with activities young adults may like and how they can translate into enjoyable adult activities to keep us active and healthy.

This also offers a chance to teach some healthy activities that may be new to the young adult such as yoga, gardening, and dancing.

In "Special Diet" we address a common theme among many adults with autism—their diet. Fortunately, special diets are much more common and accepted today, making them easier to follow. Our approach as mentors is to help our young adults (and others!) to better understand why people eat differently. This can open up discussions about food sensitivities, food allergies, and overall healthy eating habits. This leads into our last section, "Smart Eating." As we age, our metabolism slows down. This may also be compounded by medications, a less active lifestyle, and other effects of advancing age. Now is the time to work on developing healthier eating habits and eating less processed foods. With this unit, if it's possible, connect with a local nutritionist to have them discuss food choices and answer questions. It's always helpful to get information from a trained professional in your community. This unit includes a game guessing the calorie count of your favorite foods, as well as a guide to planning healthy menus with foods that you like. As a take-away with this unit we have included nutritional guidelines from a nutritionist and samples of fresh fruit or healthy gluten-free protein bars as examples of more healthy eating choices.

This is a fun unit as every topic applies to everyone in life and sometimes it's reassuring to know others have similar habits and issues. We are all together as we travel through life and hopefully the following units will help us better understand our similarities and remind us that our differences are smaller than we think.

HEALTHY NUMBERS

Hi, my name is Chris and I have autism. I am 27 years old and a big guy. I like to go to the movies and amusement parks to ride on all the rides. Sometimes the seats are too small for me and walking around the park can make me tired. So I have decided to get healthy! The first thing to do is measure my height and weight. I like numbers, but I don't care what these numbers are—I am going to use them as a starting point. Doctors also use these numbers to calculate my BMI (body mass index). That is a number that doctors use to determine how much stress I may be putting on my lungs and heart. So, as I work to get healthy I can track my progress by looking at my numbers. Are they going up or down? What are your numbers?

– GLOSSARY –

BODY MASS INDEX (BMI): This determines the amount of body fat based on a person's height and weight. It is used by doctors to help evaluate the stress on your heart and lungs.

HEART: Organ that pumps blood throughout your body.

LUNGS: Pair of organs that pump air through your body, spreading oxygen and removing carbon dioxide.

HEALTHY: Having a weight that is in the right range for my height and age. I am able to walk and move with running out of breath or tiring out.

- ACTIVITY -

Using a calculator, fill in your numbers and figure out your BMI for a start on a healthy lifestyle.

Weight: _____ lbs.   Height: _____" = _____' _____"

Height x Height = Height^2 _____" x _____" = _____"

Weight / Height^2 x 703 = BMI   _____ ÷ _____ x 703 = _____

BMI = _____ (Check table) ⟶

BMI	
Underweight	Below 18.5
Normal	18.5 – 24.9
Overweight	25.0 – 29.9
Obesity	30.0 and Above

Reprinted from the U.S. Dept. of Health and Human Services / National Institute of Health

AN ACTIVE LIFESTYLE

Hi, my name is Frances and I am friends with Chris. To help him get healthy, we have started going for walks together and working out at the gym. Part of getting healthy is moving around. Some ways to add movement to your day are taking brisk walks for 15 to 30 minutes, doing yard work, gardening, bicycling, or dancing to music. It is fun to try out the different machines at the gym and find your own favorite way to move! Sometimes you can't get out of the house or don't belong to a gym. There are some great activities you can do inside, like basic exercises and yoga. Any time you exercise, your body releases endorphins. Let's check out some basic exercises and yoga poses. Pick your favorites and try to do it at least 4 or 5 times a week. It's always fun to get healthy with a friend, so look around and find a friend to work out with you!

- GLOSSARY -

ENDORPHINS: The "happy hormone"; a group of hormones that are released by your brain during physical exercise that makes you feel relaxed and happy.

YOGA: A practice originating in ancient India which includes breathing control, meditation, and specific body poses. Yoga is great for overall health and relaxation.

WORKING OUT: When someone exercises to improve their strength, fitness, and overall health.

- ACTIVITY -

Using the pictures of six basic poses, try them out and remember to stretch.

Practice the six yoga poses. Longest held pose: _____ seconds

Favorite pose: _____

Notes on my favorite activities that help to keep me healthy:

Include favorite sports you participate in, daily walks or bike rides, gym activities, and outdoor work or play.

Basic Yoga Poses:

Easy Pose

Upward
Salute
Pose

Legs up the Wall Pose

Big Toe Pose

Cat Pose

Extended Puppy Pose

_____

_____

_____

_____

_____

_____

_____

_____

A SPECIAL DIET

Hi, my name is Luke and I am on the autism spectrum. I was getting headaches a lot, so I talked with my doctor and we decided to take gluten out of my diet. Once I stopped eating gluten, I got fewer headaches. This is how I learned that my diet affects how I feel! If I eat too much sugar I get really excited and feel like I am speeding around, but then I get really tired. If I drink cow's milk (with the protein casein), my brain gets foggy and I can't think well. If I eat a lot of bread, my ears get red and burn and sometimes I get a stomachache and a headache. Everybody is different, how do foods affect you?

– GLOSSARY –

HEADACHES: A dull, achy pain in your head which can because of diet imbalance, illness, or stress.

GLUTEN: A mixture of proteins found in flour made of wheat, barley, rye, and oats.

WHEAT: Wheat is used in making many breads and pasta.

GLUTEN FREE (GF): Breads and pastas made from products like rice, quinoa, or potatoes. They do not contain wheat and are GF (gluten free).

CASEIN: A protein found in cow's milk. Casein is not found in rice, soy, or almond milk.

- ACTIVITY -

Do you have a special diet? What are your favorite foods? What are some healthy food choices for you?

Special diet: _____

Favorite foods:

_____

_____

_____

Healthy food choices:

_____

_____

_____

SMART EATING

My name is Susie, and I have spent a lot of time reading food labels, checking on how many calories are in my food, and trying to have a healthy diet. It seems like I have been on a diet for a long time, so I have learned a few things I can share with you. When you eat, you take in calories (cal) from proteins and carbohydrates. Then, during your day, you burn calories by walking, working, exercising, and even sleeping! As an adult you stop growing, so the calories (cal) you eat need to be about equal to the calories (cal) you use during the day, or you can gain weight. So, let's look at the food you eat during the day and compare it to your activities during the day to see how it equals out!

– GLOSSARY –

NUTRITIONAL LABEL: The label on all packaged food that gives nutritional information on calories (cal), proteins, carbohydrates, and other important information.

CALORIE (CAL): A unit of energy and how we measure the energy our body needs to function. You get calories by eating food and use up calories in daily activities such as walking, working, and sleeping.

PROTEIN: Amino acids, a complex substance found in some foods that are necessary for good health. They help our body grow and repair itself. Some examples are eggs, fish, beef, chicken, beans, and cheese.

CARBOHYDRATES: Foods that break down to starches and sugars used by the body for energy. Some examples are bread, pasta, fruit, potatoes, and vegetables.

FATS: The fats and oils found in your diet. Butter, oils, and fats should be limited in a healthy diet.

DAIRY: These are foods high in calcium. Some examples are milk, ice cream, and cheeses.

HEALTHY DIET: A healthy diet means eating nutritious foods like fruits, vegetables, carbohydrates, and proteins. You may include dairy (if you can tolerate it) and small amount of fats in a healthy diet.

- ACTIVITY -

What does your daily diet look like? Remember to include both food and drinks!

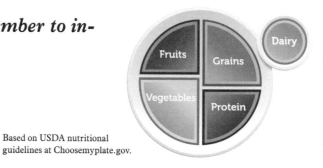

Based on USDA nutritional guidelines at Choosemyplate.gov.

Breakfast: _____

Lunch: _____

Dinner: _____

Snacks: _____

Now, using a calorie-counting book or your computer, how many calories (cals) do you eat in a day? A healthy daily diet is about 2,000 calories a day.

Breakfast: _____ calories   Dinner: _____ calories

Lunch: _____ calories   Snacks: _____ calories

Total for one day: _____ calories

Now, how can you make healthier choices to eat a balanced diet?

_____

_____

_____

_____

_____

_____

- ACTIVITY -

Let's look at some nutritional labels and learn how to read them!

What is the serving size of this food? _____

How many grams of protein is in one serving? _____

Is there any Vitamin C in this serving? _____

How many calories are in one serving? _____

Is there any fat in this container? _____

Is there any sugar in this container? _____

Is there any calcium in this container? _____

Nutrition Facts
Serving Size: 1 CONTAINER (8oz)

Amount Per Serving	
Calories 130	Fat Cal 0

	% Daily Value*
Total Fat 0g	0%
Sat Fat 0g	0%
Trans Fat 0g	
Cholest <5mg	2%
Sodium 180mg	8%
Potassium 460mg	13%
Total Carb 25g	8%
Fiber 0g	0%
Sugars 22g	
Protein 8g	16%

Vitamin A 10%	•	Vitamin C 0%
Calcium 30%	•	Iron 2%
Vitamin D 25%		

* Percent Daily Values are based on a 2,000 calorie diet

Fantastic! Let's try one more nutritional label.

What is the serving size of this food? _____

Is there any calcium in this food? _____

How many grams of protein are in one serving? _____

Is there any sugar in this food? _____

Is there any fat in this food? _____

Is there any fiber in this food? _____

Nutrition Facts
Serving Size 3 cookies

Amount Per Serving	
Calories 160	Calories from Fat 58

	% Daily Value*
Total Fat 7g	11%
Saturated Fat 2g	10%
Trans Fat 0g	
Cholesterol 0mg	0%
Sodium 190mg	8%
Potassium 0mg	0%
Total Carbohydrate 25g	8%
Dietary Fiber 1g	4%
Sugars 14g	
Protein 2g	4%

Vitamin A 0%	•	Vitamin C 0%
Calcium 0%	•	Iron 10%

* Percent Daily Values are based on a 2,000 calorie diet. Your daily values may be higher or lower depending on your calorie needs.

Now that you know how to read labels, you can work on eating healthy!

NOTES AND SUGGESTIONS

How we present ourselves to the world establishes how people see us; that's how people who don't know us start to build their perception of us. When we dress in a fun, relaxed manner, people will think we're having a casual day. If we dress in a fancy dress or a suit, it might be assumed we are off to a formal affair. That first impression can be very important and can make the path in front of us easier or harder. In this unit, we hope to open up discussions about our personal presentations, appropriate dress, and putting forth a positive, appropriate image to the world.

In "Good Hygiene" we discuss the real basics of presentation: cleanliness and good personal hygiene. These topics are often ignored or glossed over to avoid embarrassment. However, everyone needs to be aware of their bodily functions, body odors, general cleanliness, and dental health. Young adults with disabilities need to be taught how to take responsibility for themselves and their bodies. Parents and caregivers also need to realize that it may take a little more time, but we need to allow our young adults to grow up and take responsibility for themselves. What they do may not be perfect, but over time they will build self-reliance as we give these young adults the right tools to take care of themselves. As a take-away from this story, you can give them fingernail kits, sample bottles of shampoo, soap, toothbrushes, and travel grooming kits.

In "Fashion Sense" we look at how to take care of our clothes. Again, we want our young adults to start accepting the responsibility of taking care of the things they need and use every day, such as their bodies and their clothes. This story helps the reader understand how to better take care of their clothes and read clothing tags.

In "Clothing Malfunction" and "Right Clothes at the Right Time" the characters in the peer stories get embarrassed or lose out on opportunities because they are dressed inappropriately. With guidance, our adults can become aware that what they wear can affect their mood, how people see them, their ability to enjoy an activity, as well as their self-esteem. The image we project is very important as we travel through life and we need to take responsibility for ourselves.

As in all our stories, the characters are a literary creation and not based on any particular person or event.

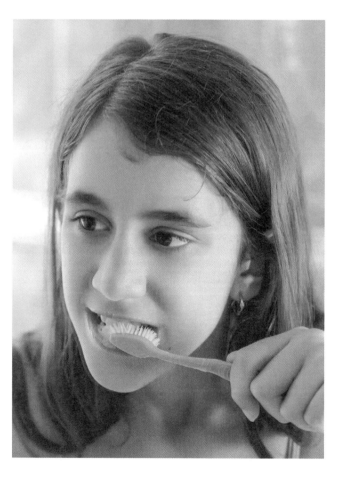
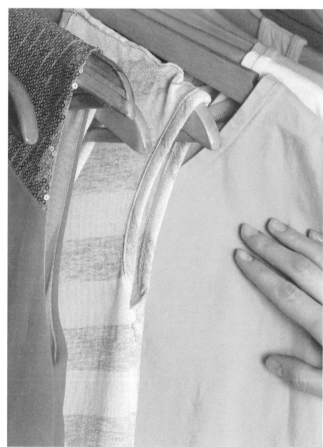

GOOD HYGIENE

Hi, my name is Mark and I am on the autism spectrum. I have a job and work hard but my co-workers have made some remarks about me not smelling very good and that my hair is greasy. That's not very nice! But when I mentioned this to my friend, he said I need to have good hygiene. I'm not even sure what he meant! I shower one day a week. I don't play in the dirt, so why do I need to shower any more than that? I don't have time in the morning and my mom always told me when to bathe, so I never really thought about it. How often should I take a bath? What about you, how often do you shower? How do you feel afterward? When do you wash your hair? How often do you cut your fingernails? How often do you get a haircut?

– GLOSSARY –

HYGIENE: A habit of body cleanliness to maintain good health and keep us from getting sick.

DEODORANT: A product that we put under our arms to prevent body odor. Some deoderants include antiperspirant to decrease sweating.

DENTAL HYGIENE: Taking care of your teeth by brushing and flossing your teeth twice daily. You should see your dentist at least once a year.

HAIR CARE: Hair needs to be shampooed at least three times a week (depending on your hair type) and styled/brushed every day. Hair needs to be cut about every two months to keep your hair healthy.

- ACTIVITY -

How's your hygiene? Do you need to make changes?

How often do you shower or take a bath per week? _____

_____

How often do you shave? _____

Do you have trouble shaving? _____

How often do you wash your hair? _____

How often do you cut your fingernails? _____

_____

How often do you get a haircut? _____

Who cuts your hair? _____

Why is it important to have good hygiene? _____

_____

Concerns: _____

_____

FASHION SENSE

Hi, my name is Ashley and I love my clothes! I like pretty dresses, skirts, blouses, cool jeans, and all the latest fashions. I don't get to go shopping a lot for new clothes because they are expensive and my parents say I don't take care of them. It's important to look good and I don't have the time to hang up my clothes or wash them—that's what my parents are for! I'll be moving out with friends soon, so who will take care of my clothes then? Can I just throw everything in the washer? How much detergent and which settings on the washing machine do I use? When the washer stops, can I throw everything into the dryer on high? Maybe I can get my mom to wash my clothes forever.

– GLOSSARY –

WASHING MACHINE OR "WASHER": A machine used to wash most clothes. Clothes should be washed after being worn for one or two days.

DRYER: A machine used to dry recently washed clothes. Use the proper settings for the types of clothes you are drying. A pair of jeans will need a higher temperature than a nice shirt.

SETTINGS: The settings on a washer or a dryer will determine the temperature of the water or heat that will be used.

 *It is always better to use cool water and low heat for most clothes.*

- ACTIVITY -

Look at your clothes and their tag to find out how to clean your clothes.

Practice with these tags:

MACHINE WASH COLD. GENTLE CYCLE. WASH WITH LIKE COLORS. ONLY NON-CHLORINE BLEACH WHEN NEEDED. TUMBLE DRY LOW. REMOVE PROMPTLY. COOL IRON IF NEEDED.

Would you wash these clothes in a washer? _____

Hot or cold water? _____

Would you put it in a dryer? _____

What temperature? _____

40°C MACHINE WASH

WARM IRON

DO NOT BLEACH

DO NOT TUMBLE DRY

WASH AND DRY DARK COLOURS SEPARATELY

Would you wash these clothes in a washer? _____

Hot or cold water? _____

Would you put it in a dryer? _____

How do you dry it? _____

CLOTHING MALFUNCTION

Yo, I'm Pete and I live in the city with my mom and sister. I like hanging out with the other guys on the street, shooting hoops, and playing on my phone. I don't pay any attention to my clothes, I just grab what I can find. I like jeans and T-shirts. I had a problem the other day when I bought some food to take home: since my hands were full, my pants kept falling down. At least I wasn't "going commando." I had on my last pair of underwear, but it was still embarrassing! I learned a lesson; I should always make sure I am dressed right before I go out and that I have a belt to keep my pants up!

THE RIGHT CLOTHES
AT THE RIGHT TIME

Hey, I'm Pete's sister, Patty. Boy, did I laugh when Pete lost his pants, and Mom was mad! Being a girl, I have the best clothes. My favorite outfit is a cute skirt and little top, and I never go anywhere without my high-heeled boots. But that was a problem when I went to an event at the gym to play basketball and do some aerobics. I had to sit out with my buddy because my high heels weren't allowed in the gym. Luckily, my buddy and I were able to take a walk outside. It was cold outside at 42°F, so I'm glad I had a coat. I guess we all need to pay attention to where we are going and what the weather will be so we don't miss out on the fun!

- GLOSSARY -

GOING COMMANDO: An expression used to describe when people go without underwear.

APPROPRIATE CLOTHING: Wearing the right clothes for the place you are going or the weather outside.

WEATHER: What is happening outside during the day or night, concerning:

COLD: Temperatures below 60°F.

WARM/HOT: Temperatures above 70°F.

HUMIDITY: The amount of moisture in the air. High humidity can make it seem warmer.

RAIN: Makes things very wet, may also be windy or stormy.

SNOW: Can make things slick or icy.

FAHRENHEIT (°F): A way of measuring temperature where water freezes at 32°F and boils at 212°F.

CELSIUS (°C): A way of measuring temperature where water freezes at 0°C and boils at 100°C.

- ACTIVITY -

Figure out which clothes you would wear for the following weather.

Spring day, 75°F, going to the park: _____

_____

_____

Fall day, 49°F, picking apples at the country farm: _____

_____

_____

Job interview, 66°F: _____

_____

_____

Hanging with friends at the gym, 54°F: _____

_____

Going swimming at the community pool, 92°F: _____

_____

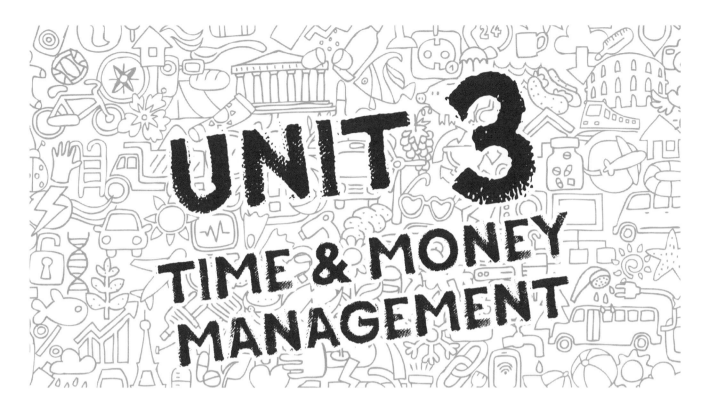

UNIT 3
TIME & MONEY MANAGEMENT

NOTES AND SUGGESTIONS

One of the most important aspects of adulthood is the ability to plan our time and enjoy our favorite activities. As we leave childhood, we have generally identified several interests that stay with us as we become adults, such as movies, video games, museums, shopping, and even certain toys. These pleasures and responsibilities should not be ignored! However, these fun activities cost money as well as time to enjoy them. In this unit, we open the discussion of scheduling your day for fun activities, work, and appointments. The starting point is the ability to tell time. Many people have trouble telling time by an analog clock (a clock face with moving hour and minute hands). Luckily, there are digital clocks, watches, and cell phones, so everyone should have a preferred method for telling time. When you are constantly asking others what time it is, it is time to get a watch!

The first story in this unit, "Scheduling Your Day," looks at a familiar theme: you are running late for an appointment, which causes stress and anxiety. The point of this story is that this particular stress can easily be eliminated with a little advanced planning. Our young adults need to understand they can assume the responsibility of planning their own days, perhaps with a little help from their families or friends. By understanding the time certain activities take to perform, you can easily plan your day with more self-responsibility and less overall stress. The day can be much more relaxed when a schedule is in place. If it is understood that you are expected to shower at 7:30 am, eat breakfast at 8:15 am, and leave by 9:00 am, then you can plan activities such as playing on the computer, checking out texts, or watching cartoons around your morning duties. Having a schedule to follow is much less stressful and more enjoyable than having someone tell you when to shower, when to dress, or when to leave the house.

The second story, "Scheduling a Fun Activity," adds the incentive of an activity in which the reader wants to participate, such as going to the movies. The reader could easily substitute another activity for this if they would prefer a trip to an amusement park, local zoo, or favorite restaurant. We also combined the scheduling aspect of the activity with managing a set amount of money. As our young adults become more responsible, they need to understand the limitations of their money and that they have the option of making certain choices based on their personal finances. With the movie example, they can make fun choices between a 3D or regular movie, large or small popcorn, or saving money for activities later. In this case, all the options are positive and still allow them the preferred activity of the movie. A wonderful take-away from this unit is actually planning a preferred activity, working out the times, money, and transportation, then engaging in the activity as planned to show how well advanced planning works.

The last story, "Planning Your Finances," opens up the conversation of what happens when you leave home. This is a common theme within families as siblings, friends, or relatives move out of the family home. This is a normal transition in many families and a perfect time to discuss finances with our young adults. Also, many of our adults are also looking at special programs, colleges, or homes when they move out of the family home and need to learn more about self-reliance as they transition into adulthood.

With adulthood comes growing responsibility and self-reliance. We hope this unit helps our young adults learn that they have the power to help plan their own future and they do not need their lives to be controlled by others. As they learn the value of time and money, their incentive to work to earn some money increases—especially if they have the ability to control how some of it is spent. As they become more aware of their potential and are allowed to take responsibility for themselves, their self-esteem will grow.

SCHEDULING YOUR DAY

Sometimes I feel like the white rabbit from *Alice in Wonderland*: "I'm late, I'm late, for a very important date!"

My name is John and I always feel like I'm going to be late, no matter where I'm going. Do you ever feel that way? I spoke with a friend and we figured out how to make a schedule by working backwards. I have to be at work by 9:00 am. Travel to work takes at least 30 minutes, so I have to leave by 8:30 am. Breakfast takes me another 30 minutes, so that puts me at 8:00 am. I also shower in the morning and it takes me about one hour (60 minutes) to take a shower, shave, brush my teeth, and get dressed. So, I need to start my morning routine at 7:00 am. If I set my alarm at 7:00 am, that will give me enough time to arrive to work at 9:00 am. I'm going to try it!

– GLOSSARY –

SCHEDULE: A plan for carrying out an activity by setting specific times and events.

ANALOG CLOCK: A clock that tells the time by moving hour and minute hands on a clock face.

DIGITAL CLOCK: A clock that tells the time by using numbers.

Which clock do you find easier to read? _____

What do you usually do when you want to know the time? _____
_____

What do you use to tell time when you are out? _____
_____

 *It is NOT good to rely on others. Everyone should have a way to tell time that they can carry with them, such as a watch or cell phone.*

- ACTIVITY -

Write out a schedule for a typical morning when you have an appointment at 10:00 am.

Activity	Amount of Time	Clock Time
Get up		
Walk into appointment		10:00 am

SCHEDULING A FUN ACTIVITY

Hi, my name is Valarie and I really enjoy going to the movies. The whole experience is fun: seeing the movie posters, buying popcorn, watching the previews in the theater, and then settling down to a great movie. The problem is, the movies are expensive; I only have limited money and I have to schedule my time so I don't miss anything. There may be a lot of people in line to buy tickets or popcorn! So, to go to a 1:00 pm movie and meet my friends, what time should I leave my house and how much money do I need?

 *Always check the time of the activity and carry a debit/credit card to make sure you have enough money for everything.*

- ACTIVITY -

The movie starts at 1:00 pm. When do you need to leave the house? Some options to remember are showering and getting dressed, eating lunch or dinner (possibly eating out), travel time, and meeting up with friends.

Activity	Amount of Time	Clock Time
Leave house		
Movie starts		1:00 pm

- ACTIVITY -

You have $30.00 for your movie experience, what do you want to buy?

Movie tickets: 2D	$10.50	3D Movie:	$14.50	IMAX Movie:	$17.50
Small Popcorn:	$5.50	Medium Popcorn:	$6.50	Popcorn Bucket:	$8.50
Water Bottle:	$4.50	Small Drink:	$4.50	Medium Drink:	$5.50
Candy Boxes:	$2.50	Nachos:	$5.50	Pretzel:	$5.50

Item	Cost	Money in Wallet
		$30.00
:	- :	=
:	- :	=
:	- :	=
:	- :	=
:	- :	=

PLANNING YOUR FINANCES

Hi everyone, my name is Angel, and I am so excited! I just got accepted to George Mason's University Life Program, so I'm going to college! There is so much to figure out. The college is about 100 miles from home so I will be living on the college campus. Honestly, I'm a little scared—but excited, too. Since I won't be living at home, I will be in charge of my own money. My folks will take care of my tuition and housing but I have to figure out how much money I will spend on food, snacks, drinks, notebooks, toiletries, and fun stuff. Will you help me? My budget is $650.00 a month. How do I make sure I have enough money for the month?

– GLOSSARY –

UNIVERSITY: Large school for students who graduate high school where they can learn a variety of subjects and earn a degree. A university may also be made up of several colleges, like the College of Science or College of Music.

COLLEGE: School that can be attended after graduating from high school.

CAMPUS: The physical location of the college or university, where students go to classes and can live in housing.

TUITION: The money paid to the college for classes.

HOUSING: Small apartments known as dormitories where students can live on campus, usually with roommates.

TOILETRIES: Items used to take care of one's body like soap, shampoo, and toothpaste.

- ACTIVITY -

With a monthly budget of $650, how should the money be divided up so I have enough for what I need? Here's Angel's budget, what is yours?

FOOD = _____ (Daily) x 30 = _____ (Monthly)

Item	Amount
Breakfast:	
Lunch:	
Dinner:	
Drinks and snacks:	

TOILETRIES = _____ (Monthly)

Item	Amount

- ACTIVITY -

MISCELLANEOUS = _____ (Monthly)

Item   Amount

_____   _____

_____   _____

_____   _____

_____   _____

_____   _____

TOTAL = _____ (Monthly): Am I over budget or within my budget?

Special Notes: _____

_____

_____

 *When away from home, remember what you NEED is more important than what you WANT. Always make sure you have food and toiletries BEFORE spending money on junk food and games.*

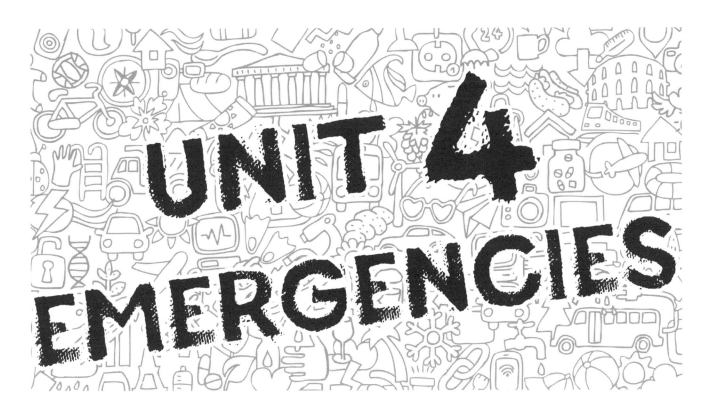

NOTES AND SUGGESTIONS

The one constant in life is that, given time, things change. That especially applies to our daily life with the possibility for of all types of accidents, mistakes, and even the weather. This unit deals with these issues, the chances of an emergency happening in our life, and how to prepare for the unexpected. We as mentors can help our young adults develop a plan so they have a support system in place when something does happen. This unit is meant to open up discussions about things that happen in life that we have little or no control over. It also gives the reader the chance to meet with local officials, such as police and firemen, to learn from these professionals as well as build a relationship with them in their own community.

The first story, "A Real Emergency?" addresses which situations are truly an emergency, as personal perspective can affect whether we classify a situation as an emergency or not. In the view of our reader, a late appointment, a missing item, or the loss of internet might constitute a personal emergency but does not rise to the level of a true emergency. The worksheet for this unit gives the reader and the mentor a chance to discuss which cases require a call to 911. However, if in doubt—and especially if the person is alone—they can ALWAYS call 911, as it is better to be safe than sorry!

As one of the worst accidents that can happen in the home, the story "Fire Safety" looks at how easy it may be to start an accidental fire and some things we can do to prevent this type of incident. As our young adults become more independent, they need to become aware of safety factors and potential dangerous situations. The kitchen is one of the most common areas for an accidental fire, so we set our story fixing breakfast. With the worksheets, our readers can discuss the components of a fire, some common fire hazards and how to prevent them, as well as how to handle a fire extinguisher. We recommend with this unit to bring in a local fire fighter to discuss fire safety as well as let the reader handle a fire extinguisher and use one in a controlled setting.

Our last story is "Natural Disasters," which discusses some of the most common natural disasters and how to prepare for them. Regardless of your geographical location, every person lives in an area that may be struck by a natural disaster such as floods, tornadoes, hurricanes, or blizzards. Everyone should be aware of the conditions preceding such a disaster and have a plan in place to protect themselves; with preparation and knowledge, a person may be able to lessen their fear and anxiety. In the worksheets we discuss the nature of various disasters and how to prepare for such an event. One suggestion is to supply an identifiable bag for each reader along with emergency preparation items so they can each create their own "disaster bag." This is a good time to have someone from a local disaster preparation agency come in to discuss how to be aware and prepared. Discussing what should go in the bag and why while putting it together yourself is much more powerful than being handed a disaster bag made by someone else.

A REAL EMERGENCY?

Hi guys. Boy, did I get in trouble last week! I was trying to get ready for my sister's graduation and everybody was acting crazy because we had to be there on time. Mom was yelling at Dad and Dad was fussing at Grandma because she was moving so slow. Susie, my sister, was yelling at me because I was playing my video game. So, I called 911 to see if we could get the police to take us to the graduation—then we could get there on time! I thought it was a good idea, but the police called our house after I called 911 and they talked to my Dad. Dad said being late isn't a "real" emergency. Can you help me figure out what *is* a real emergency?

– GLOSSARY –

EMERGENCY: A serious and often dangerous situation requiring immediate action by a professional.

911: The number that can be called from any phone to get help from the police, firemen, or medics in case of an emergency (in the USA).

POLICE: The people responsible for maintaining public order and safety.

 *Call 911 when you need help. Remember to tell them your name, address, and what the problem is so they can send the right kind of help.*

UNIT **4** EMERGENCIES

- ACTIVITY -

Determine if each event is a real emergency, why or why not, and what you should do.

Then think of some other events that might happen. Are they emergencies? Why?

Event	Is it an emergency?	Why?
Power outage		
Someone passes out		
Fire in kitchen		
Transportation is late		
Stranger in house		
Involved in or see car accident		

FIRE SAFETY

Hi everyone, my name is Matthew and I live in my own apartment. I really like having my independence and living alone. Unfortunately, when things break there's no one around to fix them and it's up to me to figure out how to take care of things. One day, I was toasting a bagel in my toaster oven when suddenly it started to smoke and smell really bad. By the time I realized it, the toaster oven had flames coming out of it! I don't know what happened; I toasted the bagel, put butter on it, and then put the bagel back in the toaster oven. What do you think happened? Do you think I should have been paying more attention to the toaster oven?

When cooking, ALWAYS stay in the kitchen and pay attention until everything is turned off and unplugged. Fire can happen quickly and is very dangerous! If there is a fire, GET OUT and call 911!

- GLOSSARY -

SMOKE: A collection of particles in the air that occur as a result of something burning. It often occurs before flames and can be more deadly, making it hard to breathe.

FIRE: The presence of flames, the visible evidence of something burning.

FIRE EXTINGUISHER: A tool that releases a substance to put out a fire.

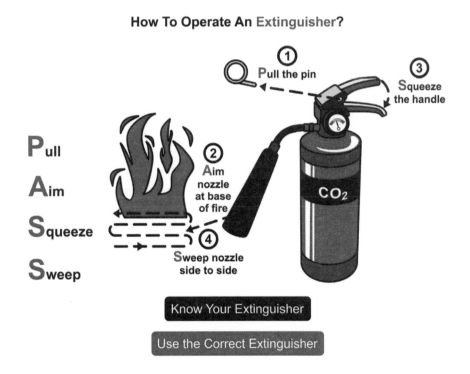

– ACTIVITY –

In the story, the buttered bagel caught fire in the toaster oven.

What was the reason for the smoke and fire? _____

How would you handle the smoke and fire? _____

What are the most common causes of fires in your home? How can you prevent them?

Fire Hazards   Preventions

_____   _____

_____   _____

_____   _____

_____   _____

NATURAL DISASTERS

Hi, my name is Martha and I was about 15 years old when we got the warning a big hurricane was coming. We prepared by stocking up on water and food that we could eat in case we didn't have electricity. We made sure we had some games, flashlights, a radio, and blankets. The storm had fierce winds and pouring rain and took down a lot of our trees. But because we were prepared, we were all safe. After the storm it took days to get our electricity back, but being safe was the most important thing. It was fun to play some games and cards and spend more time outside cooking on the grill. Even a disaster can bring people together.

– GLOSSARY –

NATURAL DISASTERS: A natural event such as a flood, earthquake, or hurricane that can cause great damage or loss of life.

HURRICANE: A violent storm originating over water with strong winds and rain.

TORNADO: A storm with strong winds that originates and moves over land.

THUNDERSTORMS: A storm with rain, thunder, and lightning.

ELECTRICITY: Electric current that is a source of power that travels through wires.

UNIT 4 EMERGENCIES

- ACTIVITY -

How would you prepare for a weather emergency?

List the items you would put in a disaster bag:

_____   _____

_____   _____

_____   _____

_____   _____

_____   _____

_____   _____

Make your own disaster bag for emergencies where you live.

NOTES AND SUGGESTIONS

People get hurt; this is a fact that we can't ignore. In this unit, the reader will recognize that everyone accidently hurts themselves at some point and it's important to know how to assess injuries and get help. This is also a good time for the reader and mentor to discuss past injuries, how they were treated, and how well they recovered so our young adults can see that people recover from most injuries with proper care and time.

In our first story, "Personal Injury," the reader may be able to identify with the girl in the story: a "klutz" who is accident-prone. It also shows the reader that when you are hurt, regardless of the injury, you should always tell a responsible adult (in this case, Mom). The glossary in this unit teaches the definition of commonly used medical terms and the worksheet gives the reader the opportunity to learn how to do a medical self-assessment and determine the extent of an injury. This knowledge should help them with their own anxiety as well as the ability to convey the extent of a medical injury to someone else. The last worksheet with this story has the reader role-playing situations handling various injuries and how to best treat the condition. This is a good time to bring in a medical professional such as a nurse, physician assistant, or an EMT. They can show the readers how to take a pulse, measure blood pressure, wrap a sprained wrist, etc.

The second story, "Accidents at Home," discusses more serious injuries at home that can result in life-threatening injuries and the need to call 911. The worksheet gives the reader the opportunity to discuss potential injuries, family members that may need help, or other accidents that necessitate calling 911.

The third story, "Too Friendly," highlights a different safety aspect: that our readers may be too friendly and not recognize appropriate social boundaries. Without appropriate social boundaries or understanding personal space, our readers may be unknowingly putting themselves in danger with strangers. The glossary discusses the differences between an acquaintance and a friend as well as personal rules. In the worksheet, the reader has the opportunity (with the guidance of the mentor) to determine their own set of personal rules, specific to the reader and their unique situation and personality. Lastly, readers build their own layered cake comprised of some of the people in their lives. Often one of the hardest layers to fill is "best friend." Either everyone is their best friend, or they have a hard time identifying a best friend. This is a great opportunity to help them identify their closest friends versus their acquaintances in their community.

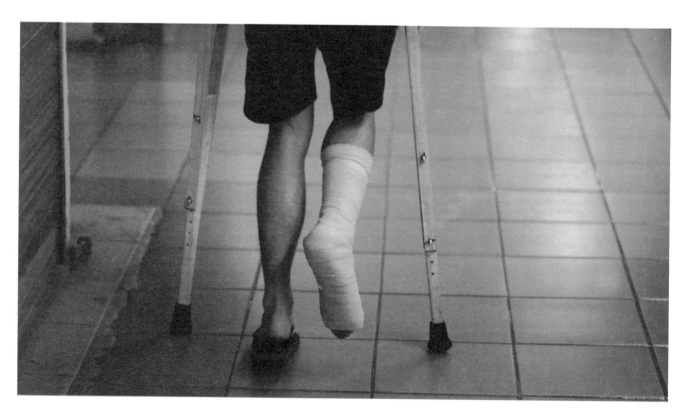

PERSONAL INJURY

Hi everyone, my name is Judy and I am sort of a "klutz!" I always seem to be falling, running into things, and generally getting in trouble. The other day I was making some soup in the microwave and it spilled when I took it out. It was so hot that I burned my finger. I wasn't sure what to do, but it hurt! I called my mom and she said to run cold water on my fingers and put on some aloe or burn medicine. It was better in just a few hours. Just yesterday I was taking my water glass downstairs, but I slipped, fell, and broke my glass. What a mess, and my ankle really hurt! I was home alone and wasn't sure what to do. What do you think I should have done?

– SELF ASSESSMENT–

Here are some questions to ask yourself when you have an accident. How do you decide what to do, especially if you are alone?

Am I bleeding? _____

Can I stop the bleeding? _____

Can I breathe? _____

Can I stand up? _____

Which part of my body hurts? _____ _____

Is anything swollen? _____

Do I think I broke a bone? _____

Do I need help? _____

Do I need to call family or a friend? ____

Do I need to call 911? _____

– GLOSSARY –

KLUTZ: A clumsy person.

SELF-ASSESSMENT: Questions you ask yourself to decide how much help you need.

NAUSEA: An upset stomach and a feeling like you are going to throw up.

VOMITING: Throwing up.

FEVER: A body temperature over 98.6°.

SPRAIN: A body joint that is hurt by an injury to the ligaments. The joint may be swollen or discolored.

BROKEN BONE: A bone which has been broken due to injury.

- ACTIVITY -

Looking at these events, how would you handle them?

Event	What would you do?
_____	_____
_____	_____
_____	_____
_____	_____
_____	_____
_____	_____
_____	_____

What similar events can you think of that might happen and what would you do?

Event	What would you do?
_____	_____
_____	_____
_____	_____
_____	_____

ACCIDENTS AT HOME

Hi, my name is Danny and I have a twin brother named David. We share a lot of thoughts as well as our likes and dislikes! The other day I was playing on the computer and my brother was outside finishing up the yard work; it was his week to cut the grass. All of a sudden, I got this really strange feeling something wasn't right and I started thinking about David and had a sudden urge to talk to him. When I got outside, my brother was on the ground with blood coming from his leg. A sharp stick had flown out of the lawn mower and hit his leg, cutting him. I was glad I found him so I could call 911 and get him help!

If someone is hurt, call 911 and they can help you. Better safe than sorry!

– ACTIVITY –

What are the some of the most common reasons to call 911?

Reasons to call 911:

_____

_____

_____

What information should you give to the 911 operator?

_____

_____

_____

Try to stay calm and stay on the line with 911 until you get help.

TOO FRIENDLY

Hi, are you friendly? I am! My name is Zoe and I would love to be your friend! Do you want to swap friendship bracelets? If you want, you can call me anytime. I love talking and texting on the phone; my number is 555-906 . . . oh yeah, my Mom says I can't give out my phone number. Sorry, sometimes, I'm not sure who I should talk to and who is a "stranger." I mean, the lady at the store is nice and so are people walking dogs. So what's wrong with being friendly? Are the rules different if someone comes to your house? Is it okay to let the delivery driver in your house? What about a stranger who needs your help? I would like to think everyone is nice, but that can be dangerous.

– GLOSSARY –

BEST FRIEND: A person you know very well, your closest friend.

FRIEND: A person you know, trust, and enjoy spending time with.

ACQUAINTANCE: A person you only know slightly, possibly from a store you go to regularly.

STRANGER: A person you do not know or have not met before.

UNIFORM: A specific set of clothes worn to symbolize a certain group or job.

PERSONAL RULES: A set of regulations you make for yourself to help you decide what to do in different situations or when you meet new people.

- ACTIVITY -

Make up your own personal rules about how to talk to new people.

_____

_____

_____

What are some things you should NEVER tell new people?

_____

_____

_____

What are some things that are okay to tell new people?

_____

_____

_____

- ACTIVITY -

Friendships in our lives are like a cake. Our best friend is the top tier, then our friends and acquaintances are the middle, and the bottom tier has the strangers in our lives. Remember, if everyone were your best friend, your cake would fall over!

List the people in your life in your friendship cake:

BEST FRIEND

FRIENDS

ACQUAINTANCES

STRANGERS

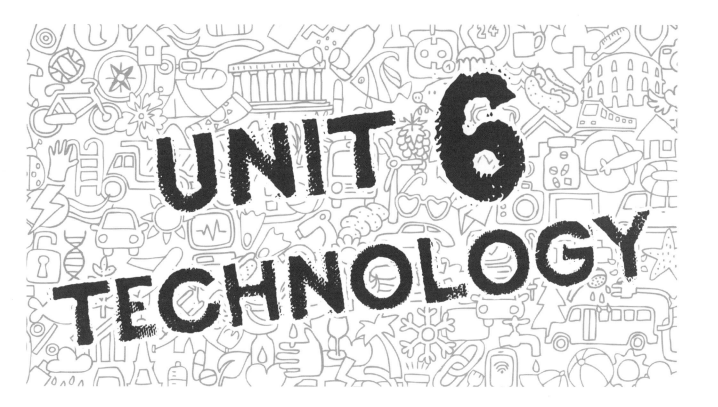

UNIT 6 TECHNOLOGY

NOTES AND SUGGESTIONS

With the advent of computers, cell phones, and smart phones, our lives have changed radically. As we—parents, care givers, and mentors—learn to use this advanced technology, we recognize that many of our children and younger adults are much more adept at browsing the web, texting, and using social networks than we may be. However, we still need to teach them the basics of using technology, such as the terminology, as well as the hazards and pitfalls of being in the "cyber community." Technology is here to stay and can be a wonderful tool for young adults, as the ability to communicate through technology can open up a whole new world for a person with autism.

The first story, "Check Out My Phone," starts with the basics of a cell phone or smart phone and the terminology associated with it as well as the etiquette associated with texting. This gives the mentor the opportunity to talk with the reader about which apps they have on their phone, which apps they may need but are not aware of (like the flashlight app), and which games they are playing. This is also a good opportunity to become more informed as to who they have been texting and the content and appropriateness of their texts. Even if the reader does not have a smart phone, the basic information about texting, games, and email can be applied to any number of internet devices used by the young adult with autism.

The next story, "Technology Frustrations," deals with the common issue of handling the frustrations that come with using the internet and video games. This is an issue that is especially relevant for our young adults with autism as many of them have varying degrees of OCD, which can compound their frustrations. This story will help the mentor address how the reader may handle stress and offer suggestions for better ways to handle their personal frustrations. Since everyone reacts to and handles stress differently, there are no right or wrong answers and we do propose several methods for handling frustrations. The wrong ways to deal with stress should also be discussed, as it is important to acknowledge if this is a problem and how to replace an inappropriate behavior with a more effective, appropriate behavior. Acknowledging an issue in a calm manner can also help a reader understand the effects that inappropriate behavior might have on those around them. Yelling and screaming at a video game in public can be very distressing to others and can result in the person being removed from the area. This is also a good time to teach alternate coping behaviors for stress. These issues are best discussed when the individual is not frustrated or stressed.

The final story, "Social Networking," deals with the pros and cons of social networking. Regardless of how we feel about social media and social networking, young adults need to be educated on how to use this platform safely. This is a good time to discuss which sites the reader likes to visit and the "netiquette" involved in using social networks. This includes the information they can safely give out, the information they should never give out, and privacy settings on social media pages. We recognize that every person and their families have their own guidelines concerning these issues and support personal preferences in these areas.

CHECK OUT MY PHONE!

Hey everyone, my name is David and I finally got my own phone! I learned that I like to text on my phone. I don't like to talk to people and texting is easier than talking. I also learned there are things I need to know about using my phone. To use your phone, you need to charge it. Remember, a dead phone is no phone, so use your charger. Also, did you know you should only text things you would be okay with ANYONE reading? That means I shouldn't text mean, angry, or sexy things. My rule is if I don't want Mom or Dad to read it, then I should not send it. My phone is also a camera and I can keep pictures on my phone, but never send naked pictures—that is known as "sexting" and can have serious consequences.

- GLOSSARY -

PHONE: An item that makes and receives calls and may also have other abilities.

TEXTING: Sending written messages or pictures to another person using a phone.

SEXTING: Sending sexual messages or naked pictures to another person using a phone. Sexting is illegal if you're underage in the US.

APPS: An "application" symbolized by an icon (pictures representing an app) that opens up a program or a game on your phone.

DEAD PHONE: A phone th at has lost its charge and will not work until re-charged.

CHARGER: A charger attaches your phone to an electrical outlet to charge it up. Different chargers work with different phones.

- ACTIVITY -

What are some of your favorite apps?

Apps I have on my phone and what they do:

_____   _____

_____   _____

_____   _____

_____   _____

What are some of the different things your phone can do?

What my phone can do: What I like doing on my phone:

_____   _____

_____   _____

_____   _____

TECHNOLOGY FRUSTRATIONS

Hi, my name is Keith and I have a sister named Terry. We love to play on the internet. My favorite thing to do is to watch movies, old cartoon clips, and funny videos on the computer. I get so frustrated when the computer slows down or freezes when I'm using it. Sometimes my internet provider is having problems and I don't know what to do, so I just start yelling.

Hi! I'm Terry, Keith's sister. I don't know why he gets so mad; he can always go play on his phone or tablet. If he wants to be really frustrated, he should try playing video games! Every time I miss a jump or get killed I have to start all over again. I'm so unlucky I can't even win a lottery spin. I never win; what can I do?

– GLOSSARY –

INTERNET: An electronic computer network that links other computer networks globally.

COMPUTER VIRUS: A bad software program that gets into a computer without your knowledge or permission. It can slow down or destroy information on your computer. Viruses can spread through the internet when you open up websites or attachments in emails.

WEBSITES: A group of webpages online.

To decrease the chance of getting a computer virus, you should only visit websites from groups you know.

- ACTIVITY -

If something isn't working right on the computer, there are some things you may want to try to fix it. This is called "troubleshooting." If there isn't a way to fix it, you must find a way to stay calm!

What frustrates you with your computer?

_____

_____

_____

_____

_____

When you become frustrated, what can you do?

_____

_____

_____

_____

_____

What are some things you can do to stay calm and not feel so frustrated?

_____

_____

_____

_____

_____

_____

Let's practice some of your suggestions. Which ones work best for you?

_____

_____

_____

_____

SOCIAL NETWORKING

I have made some of my best friends on Facebook. What about you? My name is Mary and I spend a lot my time on my computer. I love going to a lot of different websites like Pinterest, YouTube, and Facebook! I have so much fun posting ideas and pictures of things and watching funny videos. On social media, I make new friends or find out what my old friends are doing. People say I need to be careful online. Maybe I need to go over the rules I learned about talking to strangers and remember a lot of strangers are reading what I post. There are a lot of good and fun things on the internet but also a lot of strangers and bad things, so be careful!

– GLOSSARY –

SOCIAL NETWORK: An online community of people who communicate with each other sharing interests and information. Some examples of social network are Facebook, Twitter, and Pinterest.

FACEBOOK: A social media website that connects people and organizations all around the world.

PINTEREST: A website that shows off pictures of people's interests, food, and ideas to share with other people.

YOUTUBE: A website where individuals or organizations can post and share videos.

- ACTIVITY -

What are the pros and cons of social media?

Pros: Cons:

_____   _____

_____   _____

_____   _____

_____   _____

_____   _____

What are some of your favorite social media sites?

_____   _____

_____   _____

_____   _____

UNIT 7 COOKING

NOTES AND SUGGESTIONS

Food is one of everyone's favorite things because it is often associated with our families and friends— especially cooking and eating meals together. Eating is one of the first pleasurable activities we enjoy from birth and the sights, smells, and tastes of food can evoke memories of our childhood and families. In this unit we hope to open up the possibility of the enjoyment of food to everyone, especially those with autism. With such a wide variety of foods available, even those on restricted or limited diets can find wonderful options to make delicious and nutritious meals. Unfortunately, many young adults with disabilities don't have the opportunity to learn to cook or explore different foods as their meals have always been prepared by parents or caregivers. With the onset of adulthood and the transition to independence, our readers need to be prepared to manage their own needs safely. In these stories we discuss kitchen safety and the importance of always cooking with an adult present, at least initially, to prevent kitchen accidents.

In "I'm Hungry," the individual is home alone, hungry, and looking for food. Since young adults may not have spent much time in the kitchen, we start with the knowledge of the basic kitchen tools. This is also a good time to determine which tools the reader may be able to use safely, such as an electric can opener or a manual can opener, a bottle opener, a hand grater, etc. It's not surprising there is a lot of confusion between a spatula for flipping pancakes and a spatula for scraping the side of a bowl! It is also important that the reader recognizes the requirement to have all the tools ready before cooking, so the worksheet has them plan out which tools they might need to make some simple dishes.

The second story, "Time to Shop at the Grocery Store," helps the reader learn about where we get our food and how to become more independent in the store. As adults, they need to become more aware of where different products are located in the store and what some of the terms used to describe foods mean. On the worksheet, we have a generalized layout of a grocery store so the reader can identify where they might find certain items. This is a good unit in which to bring in floor maps of the reader's local grocery store and then plan a trip to go shopping.

Finally, in "Cooking Safely" the reader gets to make a basic sandwich. We make a tuna fish sandwich in this story, which can easily be substituted to a chicken salad sandwich or even a deli sandwich with cold cuts. Our other option is a grilled cheese, which gives our reader the opportunity to use a griddle and flip their own sandwich. With any recipe, we begin by making sure we have the proper kitchen tools, the foods we want (where the reader can express their creativity), and then—with supervision—they can make their own lunch.

When working with our young adults, we have to remember the lesson is not to get the "correct" answer or do something the exact same way we might do it, but to let them learn how to be themselves and succeed in their own way safely. We often use pizza cutters or small scissors for our readers who aren't able to use knives safely. We also have readers who are very proficient with knife and cutting skills because of their OCD; until you let them try, you never know how well they will do. Everyone should have the opportunity to enjoy buying, cooking, and eating good food and we hope this will be the start of enjoyable hours together in the kitchen!

I'M HUNGRY!

Hi! My name is Mike. I was just hanging out at home when my stomach started growling and I realized I was really hungry. My mom was out running errands and Dad was off working. I didn't know what to do! I decided to take a computer break and see what was in the kitchen. Well, I found some bread, a little lettuce, some mayonnaise, relish, and cheese. I remembered Mom was going to pick up more groceries, so there's not much at home. In the pantry I found some beans, potato chips, and a couple of cans of tuna. What can I make? I love a good tuna fish sandwich, so I decided to make that. I got the bread, mayo, relish, and tuna and I am ready to go.

I've got a problem! How do I open the tuna fish? It does not have a pop top, and I have never used a can opener. I'm not even sure what one looks like. I looked around and discovered an electric can opener on the counter and, luckily, figured out how to open my tuna can. It was tricky, but once I got it I was ready to make my sandwich. Do you know how to use a can opener? It can be an important tool in the kitchen and it kept me from starving! Try out these worksheets and see which kitchen tools you are familiar with.

– GLOSSARY –

 BLENDER: A machine that is used to blend soft foods or liquids, like a smoothie.

 FOOD PROCESSOR: A machine used to chop, mix, or liquefy foods.

 MIXER: An electrical tool used to mix ingredients in a bowl.

 ELECTRIC CAN OPENER: A machine to open cans.

 CAN OPENER: A tool used to open cans.

 BOTTLE OPENER: A simple tool used to take caps off of some bottles.

 FRYING PAN: A pan used to fry or cook food.

 STOCK POT: A large pot usually used to cook foods or boil water for pasta.

 TONGS: A tool used to pick things up.

 RUBBER SPATULA: A tool used to scrape food from the side of the bowls/pans.

SPATULA: A tool used to flip foods like pancakes, eggs, etc.

 MIXING BOWLS: Large bowls used to mix ingredients together.

 MEASURING CUPS: Either one cup or several different cups marked with specific amounts used in cooking or baking.

 CUTTING BOARDS: Flat boards, usually either plastic or wood, used to cut food on.

 POT HOLDERS: Heavy cloth pads used to handle hot pans to prevent burning your hands.

 *You should always have pot holders around when you cook to prevent burning your hands on hot pots or pans. Never leave pot holders on the stove because they can catch fire if put on a hot burner.*

- ACTIVITY -

Can you identify these kitchen tools? Use the glossary to check the definition. Do you know how to use them? Do you have any of these in your house?

_____ _____ _____ _____

_____ _____ _____ _____

_____ _____ _____ _____

_____ _____ _____

UNIT 7 COOKING

- ACTIVITY -

Think about these activities in the kitchen. Which tools would you need?

Make a fruit smoothie: _____

Make pancake mix: _____

Cook pancakes: _____

Make scrambled eggs: _____

Make a grilled cheese sandwich: _____

Make a tuna fish sandwich: _____

Heat up a can of soup: _____

Make boxed macaroni and cheese: _____

– TIME TO SHOP AT THE GROCERY STORE –

My name is Marie, and I love food—buying it, cooking it, and especially eating it! I grew up grocery shopping with my mom and that was always a fun trip, but now as an adult I realize it is a lot more complicated to buy food than I thought. When I go shopping I need a list or I forget things, and sometimes I can't find the food I want. What is the "produce department," anyway? Then, once I find the food, there are a lot of decisions to be made. For example, just to buy a can of tuna fish there are different brands, some in oil and some in water, some on sale, and it gets so confusing. There are even more options when shopping, such as organic, natural, GMO, vegan, and gluten-free. After talking to my mom, I learned that some choices are made because of my gluten-free diet. Some choices I get to make, like tuna with oil or tuna with water. I learned I like to buy two similar things and try them out so I can learn which brands and flavors I like! Even though it can be overwhelming, with a list and some patience I still like going grocery shopping because I can find so many good choices and healthy, fresh food!

– GLOSSARY –

ORGANIC: Food that has been been certified to be pesticide- and toxin-free.

NATURAL: Food with no artificial flavors, colors, or ingredients.

GMO: Stands for "genetically modified organisms"; non-GMO is food that has not been altered to cause the ingredient(s) to grow faster, bigger, or stay fresh longer.

MSG: Stands for "monosodium glutamate"; an additive to enhance flavor.

WHOLE GRAIN: When the entire grain is used, including parts of the kernel that contain the most nutrients.

MULTIGRAIN: When several types of grain are used.

PRODUCE: Fruits and vegetables.

DAIRY: Foods such as milk, cheese, sour cream, yogurt, and butter.

DELI: A place the has cold meats, cheese, slaws, and often hot prepared foods.

BAKERY: A place that sells a variety of cakes and breads.

PHARMACY: A place that sells personal needs items, hygiene products, and medications.

- ACTIVITY -

Using the map of the grocery store, where would you find the following items?

Blueberries: _____

Fresh fish: _____

Bandages: _____

Milk: _____

Frozen waffles: _____

Cupcakes: _____

Frozen dinner: _____

Canned tuna: _____

Hot fried chicken: _____

American cheese: _____

– COOKING SAFELY –

I'm hungry, I have my ingredients, and now I'm ready to cook!

Hi, my name's Joey. I want to cook but I am on the autism spectrum, so sometimes I need some help to cook safely. The best way to learn how to cook is to try a cooking class or have someone help you prepare meals in your home. I am going to make a grilled cheese sandwich for the adult working with me and a tuna fish sandwich for myself. Ready? For the tuna fish sandwich I need bread, mayo, tuna fish, relish, and lettuce. I like relish and lettuce but if you don't, you can leave it out. What else do I need? I need a can opener for the tuna, a bowl and fork for mixing, a knife to spread it on the bread, and a plate to eat on. If I want to toast my bread, I will need a toaster. What do we need for the grilled cheese? I need bread, butter, and cheese. The kitchen tools I need are a knife to spread the butter on the bread, a frying pan, a spatula to flip the sandwich, and a plate to eat on. So, find an adult and let's make lunch!

 *Before you cook anything, always have an adult present to help you as cooking can be dangerous.*

- GLOSSARY -

INGREDIENTS: The items need to make a certain recipe.

BAKING: To cook food in an oven.

BOILING: To cook food in water that has been heated until it is bubbling and turning to steam.

FRYING: To cook food in a small amount of hot oil, usually in a shallow pan.

DEEP FRYING: To cook food by submerging it entirely in hot oil in a deep pan.

BROILING: To cook food by applying heat on the top of the food only.

TOASTING: To cook food by applying heat on the top and bottom of food at the same time (i.e., toasted bread).

When you are finished cooking, ALWAYS remember to unplug or turn off all cooking tools such as burners, ovens, toasters, toaster ovens or electric skillets. Never leave the kitchen if you are cooking!

- ACTIVITY -

With adult supervision, make your lunch. You can try these recipes or come up with one of your own. Have fun, be safe, and happy eating!

Recipe for TUNA FISH SANDWICH:

Ingredients:

Can of tuna fish

Mayonnaise

Pickle relish (optional)

Lettuce (optional)

Bread (2 slices)

Tools Needed:

Can opener

Mixing bowl

Spoon/fork

Measuring spoon (1 tablespoon)

Toaster (optional)

Directions:

1. Open can of tuna, drain oil/water, and put the meat into a mixing bowl.

2. Add 2 to 3 tablespoons of mayonnaise and 1 tablespoon of pickle relish, then mix.

3. Toast bread if desired, add lettuce (if desired) to bread, cover with tuna fish mixture, put on your plate, and enjoy!

Recipe for GRILLED CHEESE SANDWICH:

Ingredients:

Cheese (American, Swiss, or cheddar)

Butter, soft

Bread (2 slices)

Tools Needed:

Frying pan or griddle

Knife

Spatula

Directions:

1. Spread soft butter on one side of each piece of the bread.

2. Place slices of the cheese on the unbuttered side of the bread.

3. Place the bread with the buttered side down in the frying pan and put the burner on the "medium" setting. Watch carefully. After a few minutes, when the bread turns light brown in color, use the spatula to flip the sandwich over to the other buttered side.

4. After a few more moments, turn off the frying pan, move it off the burner, and remove sandwich. Place it on a plate and enjoy!

WORKSHEET EXAMPLES

UNIT 1

"HEALTHY NUMBERS" EXAMPLE

- ACTIVITY -

Chris' height is 5'10" and his weight is 185 lbs. These are his calculations. Using a calculator, fill in your numbers and figure out your BMI for a start on a healthy lifestyle.

Weight: _185_ lbs.

Height: _70"_ = _5'_ _10"_

Height x Height = Height^2 _70_ " x _70_ " = _4900_ "

Weight / Height^2 x 703 = BMI   _185_ ÷ _4900_ x 703 = _26.5_

BMI = _26.5_ (Check table) ➡

BMI	
Underweight	Below 18.5
Normal	18.5 – 24.9
Overweight	25.0 – 29.9
Obesity	30.0 and Above

Reprinted from the U.S. Dept. of Health and Human Services / National Institute of Health

"AN ACTIVE LIFESTYLE" EXAMPLE

- ACTIVITY -

Using the pictures of six basic poses, try them out and remember to stretch.

These are Frances' answers. What are yours?

Practice the six yoga poses. Longest held pose: _25_ seconds

Favorite pose: Extended Puppy Pose

Notes on my favorite activities that help to keep me healthy:

(Include favorite sports you participate in, daily walks or bike rides, gym activities, and outdoor work or play.)

Walking on the treadmill	Going to the amusement park
Swinging at the park	Dancing class
Bowling with friends	Walking around the zoo
Swimming at the pool	Bicycling with friends

"A SPECIAL DIET" EXAMPLE

- ACTIVITY -

These are Luke's answers. What are yours? Do you have a special diet? What are your favorite foods? What are some healthy food choices for you?

Special diet: _GFCF (Gluten free/casein free) diet: no wheat and no cow's milk_

Favorite foods:

Dairy-free ice cream	GF cereal
Hamburger	Apples and grapes
Spaghetti with GF pasta	Chicken and rice

Healthy food choices:

Oranges	GF protein bars
Mixed green salads	Adding lettuce and tomato to hamburger
Broccoli and carrots	Drinking water

"SMART EATING" EXAMPLE

- ACTIVITY -

Here's Susie's daily diet as an example. What is yours?

What does your daily diet look like? Remember to include both food and drinks!

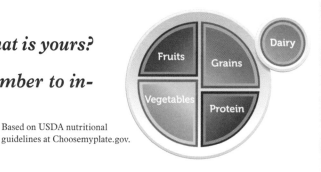

Based on USDA nutritional
guidelines at Choosemyplate.gov.

Breakfast: Half a bagel with cream cheese, grapes, and orange juice

Lunch: Tuna fish sandwich with potato chips and a glass of milk

Dinner: Meatloaf, mashed potatoes, and green beans with unsweetened iced tea

Snacks: Bowl of popcorn, an apple, a bowl of ice cream

Now, using a calorie-counting book or your computer, how many calories (cals) do you eat in a day? A healthy daily diet is about 2,000 calories a day.

Breakfast: 350 calories   Dinner: 500 calories

Lunch: 750 calories   Snacks: 400 calories

Total for one day: 2,000 calories

Now, how can you make healthier choices to eat a balanced diet?

Salads instead of french fries, water instead of soda
_____

Fix meals at home instead of having fast food or frozen meals
_____

More fruits and vegetables, less bread and chips
_____

_____

_____

_____

- ACTIVITY -

Let's look at some nutritional labels and learn how to read them!

What is the serving size of this food? *1 container, 8oz = 1 cup*

How many grams of protein is in one serving? *8 grams*

Is there any Vitamin C in this serving? *No*

How many calories are in one serving? *130 calories*

Is there any fat in this container? *No*

Is there any sugar in this container? *Yes, 22 grams = 5 ½ teaspoons*

Is there any calcium in this container? *Yes, 30% of our daily value*

Nutrition Facts
Serving Size: 1 CONTAINER (8oz)

Amount Per Serving	
Calories 130	Fat Cal 0

	% Daily Value*
Total Fat 0g	0%
Sat Fat 0g	0%
Trans Fat 0g	
Cholest <5mg	2%
Sodium 180mg	8%
Potassium 460mg	13%
Total Carb 25g	8%
Fiber 0g	0%
Sugars 22g	
Protein 8g	16%

Vitamin A 10%	•	Vitamin C 0%
Calcium 30%	•	Iron 2%
Vitamin D 25%		

*Percent Daily Values are based on a 2,000 calorie diet

Fantastic! Let's try one more nutritional label.

What is the serving size of this food? *3 cookies*

Is there any calcium in this food? *No*

How many grams of protein are in one serving? *2 grams, 4% of our daily value (DV)*

Is there any sugar in this food? *14 grams = 3 ½ teaspoons*

Is there any fat in this food? *7 grams, 11% DV*

Is there any fiber in this food? *1 gram, 4% DV*

Nutrition Facts
Serving Size 3 cookies

Amount Per Serving	
Calories 160	Calories from Fat 58

	% Daily Value*
Total Fat 7g	11%
Saturated Fat 2g	10%
Trans Fat 0g	
Cholesterol 0mg	0%
Sodium 190mg	8%
Potassium 0mg	0%
Total Carbohydrate 25g	8%
Dietary Fiber 1g	4%
Sugars 14g	
Protein 2g	4%

Vitamin A 0%	•	Vitamin C 0%
Calcium 0%	•	Iron 10%

*Percent Daily Values are based on a 2,000 calorie diet. Your daily values may be higher or lower depending on your calorie needs.

Now that you know how to read labels, you can work on eating healthy!

UNIT 2

"GOOD HYGIENE" EXAMPLE

- ACTIVITY -

As an example, here are Mark's answers:

How often do you shower or take a bath per week? I shower every morning Monday. through Friday and maybe once during the weekend.

How often do you shave? Every morning after my shower.

Do you have trouble shaving? Sometimes I miss certain spots, but I like using shaving cream!

How often do you wash your hair? Every time I shower, about six times a week.

How often do you cut your fingernails? Every two weeks, but sometimes I need help with my toenails.

How often do you get a haircut? I get my hair cut every two to three months.

Who cuts your hair? My mom used to cut it but now I go to a barber in my neighborhood.

Why is it important to have good hygiene? I like to look and smell good when I go out. It gives me self-confidence when I meet people. Good hygiene also helps me to feel good and not get sick.

Concerns: _____

_____

"FASHION SENSE" EXAMPLE

- ACTIVITY -

Look at your clothes and their tag to find out how to clean your clothes.

Practice with these tags:

MACHINE WASH COLD. GENTLE CYCLE. WASH WITH LIKE COLORS. ONLY NON-CHLORINE BLEACH WHEN NEEDED. TUMBLE DRY LOW. REMOVE PROMPTLY. COOL IRON IF NEEDED.

Would you wash these clothes in a washer? _Yes_

Hot or cold water? _Cold water_

Would you put it in a dryer? _Yes_

What temperature? _Low temperature_

40°C MACHINE WASH

WARM IRON

DO NOT BLEACH

DO NOT TUMBLE DRY

WASH AND DRY DARK COLOURS SEPARATELY

Would you wash these clothes in a washer? _Yes_

Hot or cold water? _40°C = 104°F is a warm water wash_

Would you put it in a dryer? _No_

How do you dry it? _Hang dry or lay on a towel_

"RIGHT CLOTHES AT THE RIGHT TIME" EXAMPLE

- ACTIVITY -

Figure out which clothes you would wear for the following weather. Here are Pete and Patty's answers:

Spring day, 75°F, going to the park: I would wear shorts or jeans with a T-shirt or short-sleeved shirt. Sandals or tennis shoes would be my choice for shoes.

Fall day, 49°F, picking apples at the country farm: I would wear jeans or maybe corduroy pants with a long-sleeved shirt. I would definitely have a jacket and either tennis shoes or boots (with no high heels).

Job interview, 66°F: I would wear a nice pair of pants (not jeans) with a dress shirt, a tie, and a nice jacket if I had one. Patty would wear a nice dress, dress pants, or a skirt with a pretty blouse. We would both wear nice shoes, maybe Patty would wear a pair with a small heel.

Hanging with friends at the gym, 54°F: Workout clothes would work well for Pete or Patty: something comfortable like gym shorts, a T-shirt, and tennis shoes.

Going swimming at the community pool, 92°F: Bathing suits and a cover-up (like shorts and a shirt) with flip-flops or sandals. Don't forget a towel!

UNIT 3

"SCHEDULING YOUR DAY" EXAMPLE

- ACTIVITY -

Here is John's personal schedule for his typical morning when he has an appointment at 10:00 am. Use this as an example and figure out your schedule.

Activity	Amount of time	Clock time
Get up		7:30 am
Computer time	30 minutes	8:00 am
Shower and shave	30 minutes	8:30 am
Brush teeth and hair	15 minutes	8:45 am
Get dressed	15 minutes	9:00 am
Breakfast	30 minutes	9:30 am
Travel time	30 minutes	10:00 am
Walk into appointment		10:00 am

"SCHEDULING A FUN ACTIVITY" EXAMPLE

- ACTIVITY -

The movie starts at 1:00 pm. When do you need to leave the house? Some options to remember are showering and getting dressed, eating lunch or dinner (possibly eating out), travel time, and meeting up with friends. This is Valarie's plan, what's yours?

Activity	Amount of time	Clock time
Leave house		11:30 am
Travel time	30 minutes	Arrive at 12:00 pm
Get tickets and popcorn	30 minutes	Finished by 12:30 pm
Watch previews and pre-show	30 minutes	Finished by 1:00 pm
Movie starts		1:00 pm

- ACTIVITY -

You have $30.00 for your movie experience, what do you want to buy?

Here are Valarie's choices. What are yours?

Movie tickets: 2D	$10.50	3D Movie:	$14.50	IMAX Movie:	$17.50
Small Popcorn:	$5.50	Medium Popcorn:	$6.50	Popcorn Bucket:	$8.50
Water Bottle:	$4.50	Small Drink:	$4.50	Medium Drink:	$5.50
Candy Boxes:	$2.50	Nachos:	$5.50	Pretzel:	$5.50

Item		Cost		Money in wallet
				$30.00
3D Movie $14.50	: -	$30.00 - $14.50	: =	$ 15.50
Medium Popcorn $6.50	: -	$15.50 - $6.50	: =	$ 9.00
Small Drink $4.50	: -	$9.00 - $4.50	: =	$4.50
Candy Box $2.50	: -	$4.50 - $2.50	: =	$2.00
	: -		: =	

"PLANNING YOUR FINANCES" EXAMPLE

- ACTIVITY -

With a monthly budget of $650, how should the money be divided up so I have enough for what I need? Here's Angel's budget, what is yours?

FOOD = ___$15___ (Daily) x 30 = ___$450___ (Monthly)

Item	Amount
Breakfast: Protein bar and orange juice	$3.00
Lunch: Sandwich, chips, and water bottle	$4.00
Dinner: Pizza and soft drink	$6.00
Drinks and snacks: Popcorn, fruit, ice cream	$2.00

TOILETRIES = ___$100___ (Monthly)

Item	Amount
Shampoo, shaving cream, and deodorant	$15.00
Personal toiletries and make-up	$25.00
Toilet paper and paper towels	$25.00
Tissues, medicines, and mouthwash	$35.00

MISCELLANEOUS = ___*$100*___ (Monthly)

Item	Amount
Notebooks and pens	$ 15.00
Batteries, chargers, and earbuds	$ 20.00
Movies and entertainment	$ 25.00
Transportation	$ 25.00
Savings/emergency fund	$15.00

TOTAL = ___*$650*___ (Monthly): Am I over budget or within my budget?

 *Everyone's budget will be different, but always try to save some money every month for emergencies. You never know what will happen in the future!*

UNIT 4

"A REAL EMERGENCY?" EXAMPLE

– ACTIVITY –

Determine if each event is a real emergency, why or why not, and what you should do.

Then think of some other events that might happen—are they emergencies? Why or why not?

These are Paul's answers. What are your emergencies? When should you call 911?

Event	Is it an emergency?	Why?
Power outage	No	Can call power company to report outage
Someone passes out	Yes	Need medical help
Fire in kitchen	Yes	Fire can spread quickly, dangerous
Transportation is late	No	Call transportation company
Stranger in house	Yes	You need to be safe, lock doors
Involved in or see car accident	Yes	People may be injured, can cause traffic

"FIRE SAFETY" EXAMPLE

– ACTIVITY –

In the story, the buttered bagel caught fire in the toaster oven.

What was the reason for the smoke and fire? *The butter dripped and started the fire*

How would you handle the smoke and fire? *Unplug the toaster, use a fire extinguisher*

What are the most common fire hazards in your home? How can you prevent them? Here are Matthew's answers. What are yours?

Fire hazards	Preventions
Appliances plugged in and turned on	Always unplug appliances
Dish towels left on the stove	Keep all paper and dish towels off of the stove
Burning food while cooking	Never leave the kitchen when the stove is on
Hot oil catches fire	Be VERY careful with hot oil, very flammable

"NATURAL DISASTERS" EXAMPLE

- ACTIVITY -

How would you prepare for a weather emergency?

This is what Martha put in her personal disaster bag. What would you put in yours?

List the items you would put in a disaster bag:

Bottle of water	Favorite snacks (not refrigerated)
Radio with batteries	Portable chargers for phones
Portable chargers for electronic games	Ear buds
Favorite toy/stuffed animal	Books/magazines
Pen, pencil, paper	Deck of cards
Board games, dice, game book	Extra towel and clothes
Can opener	Medicine
Medical kit	Hand sanitizer

Make your own disaster bag for emergencies where you live.

UNIT 5

"PERSONAL INJURY" EXAMPLE

- ACTIVITY -

Looking at these events, how would you handle them?

Event	What would you do?
A burn on your finger from touching a hot pan	Run cold water on burn
You feel dizzy when you get up	Sit down immediately and call someone for help
Stomachache	Drink clear liquids, eat crackers or something light
Stomachache and vomiting	Drink clear liquids until vomiting stops
Fever (temperature over 98.6°F)	Call someone, go see a doctor
Small cut (bleeding can be stopped)	Stop bleeding, bandage, tell someone
Large cut (bleeding can NOT be stopped)	Pressure on cut, call someone, see doctor
Fall that results in a swollen joint	Call someone, see doctor

 *If you hurt yourself, always tell someone. It is also a good idea to see a doctor or medical professional and have them check out your injury. Better to be safe and healthy!*

"ACCIDENTS AT HOME" EXAMPLE

- ACTIVITY -

What are the some of the most common reasons to call 911?

Here are some answers about calling 911. What are your answers?

Reasons to call 911:

Someone has fallen, gotten hurt, and needs help

Fire breaks out in the house and you don't know what to do

What information should you give to the 911 operator?

Your name

What the problem is

Your address

If you have a disability, tell the 911 operator

Try to stay calm and stay on the line with 911 until you get help.

"TOO FRIENDLY" EXAMPLE

- ACTIVITY -

Make up your own personal rules about how to talk to new people.

Always say "hi" when you meet a new person, but don't talk too much about yourself.

You can compliment someone on something they are wearing by saying things like "nice jewelry" or "pretty shirt."

What are some things you should NEVER tell new people?

Never tell new people personal things about your family, money, or personal problems.

Never give or ask a new friend for money, personal things, or a favor.

What are some things that are okay to tell new people?

Tell them how happy you are to meet them.

Compliment them on something.

Look for common interests like movies, games, and places you have been.

- ACTIVITY -

Friendships in our lives are like a cake. Our best friend is the top tier, then our friends and acquaintances are the middle, and the bottom tier has the strangers in our lives. Remember, if everyone were your best friend, your cake would fall over!

List the people in your life in your friendship cake:

BEST FRIEND
ASHLEY

FRIENDS
CHRIS, ANGEL, FRANCES, MARK

ACQUAINTANCES
MARY, WHO I SEE WEEKLY AT THE GYM; JULIE, WHO CUTS MY HAIR;
JOHN, MY BOSS AT WORK

STRANGERS
THE DELIVERY GUY, THE POSTMAN, PEOPLE AT THE STORE,
PEOPLE AT THE MALL, PEOPLE AT THE PARK

UNIT 6
"CHECK OUT MY PHONE!" EXAMPLE

- ACTIVITY -

What are some of your favorite apps?

Here are some phone apps. What is on your phone?

Apps I have on my phone and what they do:

Messages (texts)

Gallery (for pictures)

Email (for email messages)

Calendar (keep track of appointments)

App store

Calculator (when I need to do math)

- ACTIVITY -

What are some of the different things your phone can do?

What my phone can do:	What I like doing on my phone:
Flashlight	Games
Weather alerts	Checking out videos
Make phone calls	Texting friends
Take pictures	Sharing pictures with friends

"TECHNOLOGY FRUSTRATIONS" EXAMPLE

- ACTIVITY -

If something isn't working right on the computer, there are some things you may want to try to fix it. This is called "troubleshooting." If there isn't a way to fix it, you must find a way to stay calm!

Here are Keith and Terry's answers. Do they look like your answers?

What frustrates you with your computer?	When you become frustrated, what can you do?
When the internet goes really slow	Reboot your computer, ask nicely for help
When the computer freezes up	Close down websites, reboot computer
When I don't get what I want on my video game	Take a break, remember it's only a game
When my battery dies	Make sure you have a charger, change the batteries

What are some things you can do to stay calm and not feel so frustrated?

Deep breaths, yoga poses	Play a different game
Get off electronics and go outside	Call or visit friends
Watch TV or a DVD while computer is down	Check out magazines, puzzles, and games

Let's practice some of your suggestions. Which ones work best for you?

Play a different game

_____

_____

_____

Deep breathing, yoga poses

_____

_____

_____

"SOCIAL MEDIA" EXAMPLE

- ACTIVITY -

What are the pros and cons of social media? Here are some answers, what are yours?

Pros:

Cons:

Can connect with old school friends

Can open my site up to strangers

Can share my thoughts and ideas

Strangers can find out personal info

Can get good ideas about food

May get a virus on my computer

Can get good arts and craft ideas

May see or read things I don't like

What are some of your favorite social media sites?

Facebook

Pinterest

YouTube

Movie websites

115

UNIT 7
"I'M HUNGRY!" EXAMPLE

- ACTIVITY -

Can you identify these kitchen tools? Use the glossary to check the definition. Do you know how to use them? Do you have any of these in your house?

can opener

stock pot

mixer

rubber spatula

bottle opener

mixing bowl

tongs

hot pad

food processor

frying pan

cutting board

spatula

electric can opener

measuring spoons

blender

- ACTIVITY -

Think about these activities in the kitchen. Which tools would you need?

Make a fruit smoothie: A blender to mix up smoothie ingredients

Make pancake mix: A mixing spoon, mixing bowls, and measuring cups

Cook pancakes: A spoon to dip in the pancake mix, a frying pan, and a spatula

Make scrambled eggs: A bowl and a fork to mix the eggs, a frying pan, and a spatula to stir the eggs in the pan and serve them

Make a grilled cheese sandwich: A knife to spread the butter on the bread, a frying pan, and a spatula

Make a tuna fish sandwich: A can opener for the tuna, a bowl for mixing, and a knife to spread the tuna

Heat up a can of soup: A can opener for the soup, a pot, and a spoon to stir

Make boxed macaroni and cheese: A pot to boil water for pasta, a strainer, a measuring cup for milk, and a spoon to stir

- ACTIVITY -

Using the map of the grocery store, where would you find the following items?

Blueberries: _Produce department_

Fresh fish: _Seafood department_

Bandages: _Pharmacy_

Milk: _Dairy department_

Frozen waffles: _Frozen foods_

Cupcakes: _Bakery_

Frozen dinner: _Frozen foods_

Canned tuna: _Center Aisles (Aisle 2)_

Hot fried chicken: _Deli_

American cheese: _Dairy department_

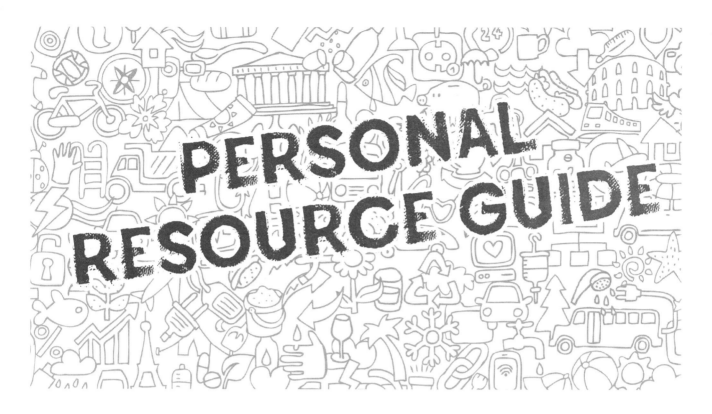

PERSONAL RESOURCE GUIDE

Fill in the following guide to help you access information you or others might need. As information changes, remember to update your guide.

Name: _____ Date of Birth: _____

Address: _____

City, State, Zip: _____

Cell phone number: _____ House phone number: _____

County/City of residence: _____

Closest relative living with you: _____ Relationship: _____

Closest relative NOT living with you: _____

Relationship: _____ Phone number: _____

Attendant / Case manager: _____

Contact info for attendant / case manager: _____

Additional information attendant / case manager: _____

_____

Job Coach: _____

Employer: _____

Supervisor & contact info: _____

Transportation contact info: _____

Phone service provider contact info: _____

Internet/cable company contact info: _____

Electric company contact info: _____

Non-emergency police numbers / 911: _____

Use this page for any additional information you want to keep.

_____

_____

_____

_____

_____

_____

_____

_____

_____

_____

_____

_____

_____

_____

_____

_____

_____

_____

_____

_____

_____

_____

_____

_____

_____

_____

_____

_____

ABOUT THE AUTHOR

Parent of a twenty-eight-year-old son with autism, Weaver's dual degrees in biology and health sciences with a certification as a physician's assistant were a strong foundation for her additional training in the early 1990s in the Lovaas method of ABA and the Greenspan Floortime methodology. She acquired additional training in TEACCH and PECS during her employment as a teacher and specialist with Henrico County School System in VA. She has over twenty years of experience working with persons with autism including the Henrico County school system, serving as the past president of the Autism Society of America-Central VA Chapter, and four years as the director of the Tuckahoe Little League Challenger Division. Additionally, she is one of the co-founders and president of the Skills Development Center (SDC), a non-profit organization founded in 2011 dedicated to the continued learning and self-empowerment of adults over eighteen with intellectual and developmental disabilities. Her passion is her current job as the program director of the SDC, working with these adults as they continue to learn skills, explore, and develop talents, and helping them connect with their peers in a facilitated recreation center at the Skills Development Center.

In 2017 she developed and wrote a workbook to be used for this population to help them learn some of the softer, subtler skills of adulthood such as technology, internet, health, hygiene, and cooking. This workbook has been used for several classes at the Skills Development Center.

Patricia Weaver

President, Program Director

pweaver@thesdc.org

DID YOU LIKE THE BOOK?

Rate it and share your opinion.

amazon.com

BARNES&NOBLE
BOOKSELLERS
www.bn.com

Not what you expected? Tell us!

Most negative reviews occur when the book did not reach expectation. Did the description build any expectations that were not met? Let us know how we can do better.

Please drop us a line at *info@fhautism.com*.

Thank you so much for your support!

FUTURE HORIZONS INC.

Keep up with the Latest Books and Conferences on Autism!

World Leader in Autism Resources

FUTURE HORIZONS INC.

Go to www.FHautism.com

And follow us on:

GET THE SECRET
OF THEIR SUCCESS

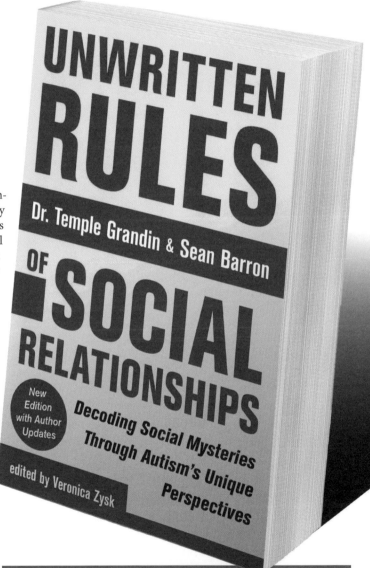

UNWRITTEN RULES

Dr. Temple Grandin & Sean Barron

OF SOCIAL RELATIONSHIPS

New Edition with Author Updates

Decoding Social Mysteries Through Autism's Unique Perspectives

edited by Veronica Zysk

Born with autism, both Temple Grandin and Sean Barron now live famously successful lives. However, their paths were quite different. Temple's logical mind controlled her social behavior. Logic informed her decision to obey social rules and avoid unpleasant consequences. Sean's emotions controlled his social behavior. Baffled by social rules and isolated, he made up his own rules, and applied them to others. When they broke his rules, he felt unloved.

Both Temple and Sean came to terms with the social world and found their places in it. Whether you are a person with autism, a caregiver, or just someone interested in an outsider view of society, their powerful stories will enlighten you.

FUTURE HORIZONS INC.
World Leader in Autism Resources

800.489.0727 | FHautism.com

$19⁹⁵ | Softcover | 448 pages